One Hour
Eighteen Minutes

By **Elena Gremina**
Translated and adapted for
performance by **Noah Birksted-Breen**

Published by Playdead Press 2012

One Hour Eighteen Minutes © Elena Gremina 2010
This translation © Noah Birksted-Breen 2012

Elena Gremina and Noah Birksted-Breen have asserted
their rights under the Copyright, Design and Patents
Act, 1988, to be identified as the author of this work.

A CIP catalogue record for this book is available from
the British Library.

ISBN 978-0-9574491-0-7

Playdead Press
www.playdeadpress.com

One Hour Eighteen Minutes was first performed on 13th of November 2012 at the New Diorama Theatre.

Cast (in alphabetical order):
Alan Francis
Wendy Nottingham
Rebecca Peyton
Danny Scheinmann

Designer	**takis**
Lighting designer	**Charlie Lucas**
Sound designer	**Ed Clarke**
Video designer	**Ben Chessell**
Fight Director	**Bret Yount**

Co-producer	**Margarita Osepyan**
Production Manager	**Tim Highman**
Assistant Director	**Elizabeth Moore**
Stage Manager	**Nina Scholar**
Costume Supervisor	**Clare Amos**
Assistant Stage Manager	**Claire Charlesworth**

Roles:
Alan Francis: Vladimir, Sergei's Voice, The Guard.
Wendy Nottingham: Natalia Nikolaevna Magnitskaya, Sergei's Colleague, Elena Stashina, Irina Dudkina.
Rebecca Peyton: Natasha Magnitskaya, Lawyer, Alexandra Gauss, Lilia, Prosecutor, Young Woman in the Ambulance, Home Office Official.
Danny Scheinmann: Police Officer, Investigating Officer (Oleg Silchenko), Sasha, Journalist.

Elena Gremina- Playwright

Elena is considered by many to be the most important political playwright in Russia. She is a member of the artistic advice board for the Festival for Young Playwrights 'Lyubimovka' (since 2007). She has been published in Moscow theatre journals and is the laureate of the Stalker Prize in 2005 for her work in contemporary theatre, the winner of the All-Russian Competition of Plays in Moscow, and winner of the best radio-play in 1991and 1993. She was commissioned by Tricycle Theatre to co-write one of the plays in The Bomb, and has been commissioned by The Royal Court. GREMINA also co-founded Teatr.doc in Moscow, which has been instrumental in fostering political play writing in Russia.

Noah Birksted-Breen- Director/Co-producer

Noah has directed seven productions in fringe and off-West End venues. He won the Channel 4 Theatre Director's Award in 2006, and was training resident director at Hampstead Theatre for eighteen months assisting directors such as Rupert Goold, Lucy Bailey and Polly Teale. In 2005 Noah founded Sputnik Theatre Company, dedicated to sourcing, translating and staging new Russia drama in the UK. Noah is Artistic Director of the Russian Theatre Festival in London.

CAST

Alan Francis- Vladimir

Theatre includes: *The Tempest* (Dundee Rep), *Twelfth Night* (RSC), *Penetrator* (Royal Court and Traverse Theatre), *Jeffrey Dahmer is Unwell* (Kings Head), *The Wonderful World of Dissocia* (Tour), *Breaker Morant* (Edinburgh Festival), *The Winters Tale* (Royal Lyceum), *Three Men in a Boat* (York Theatre Royal), *Caledonia* (National Theatre of Scotland), *Accolade* (Finsborough Theatre). Television includes: *Alistair McGowan's Big Impression, The 11 O'Clock Show* (Channel 4), *Pulling* (BBC), *Taggart* (ITV). Radio includes: *Stamp Collecting with Legs, It's that Jo Caulfield Again* and *Inside Alan Francis* (All BBC Radio 4). Alan was in two shows at the Edinburgh Festival this year: *Mid Morning Matters* (Baby Cow) and *Alan Francis: Expands* (Gilded Balloon).

Wendy Nottingham- Natalia Magnitskaya
Theatre includes: *Celebrity Night at Cafe Red* and *Step 9 of 12* (Trafalgar Studios), *In Basildon* (Royal Court), *Grief* (National Theatre), *Fen* (Finborough), *Stoopud Fucken Animals* (Traverse Theatre), *Cloud Nine* (Crucible Theatre), *Abigail's Party* (Hampstead/ Ambassadors Theatre), *The York Realist* (Tour/Royal Court), *It's A Great Big Shame!* (Stratford East). Film includes: *Bigga Than Ben* (Bigga Than Ben), *Notes On A Scandal* (Fox Searchlight), *Babel* (GHM Films), *Vera Drake, Topsy-Turvy* and *Secrets and Lies* (Thin Man Films), *The Short and Curlies* (Portman Quintet). Television includes *Mr Selfridge* (ITV), *The Borgias* (LB TV Productions), *A Young Doctor's Notebook* (BigTalk), *Victoria Wood Christmas Special* (BBC), *Getting On* (BBC), *Spooks* (Kudos), *Housewife 49* (Granada), *People Like Us* (BBC), *The Peter Principle* (Hatrick), *The Sculptress* (Red Rooster), *Precious Bane* (BBC).

Rebecca Peyton- Natasha Magnitskaya
Theatre includes: *Enduring Song* (Bristol Old Vic), *Billy Chickens is a Psychopath Superstar* (Theatre 503/Latitude), *The Odyssey* (The Albany, Deptford), *Soldiers* (Finborough Theatre), *Hothouse* (Arcola Theatre & tour), *Troubleshooters* (Soho Theatre), *Julius Caesar* (Barbican), *Electra* (The Gate), Danelaw (White Bear), Next Door (Rosemary

Branch), *La Bête Humaine* (Grange Court Theatre), *Here But There* (Teatro Vivo tour), *Two* (Judi Dench Theatre). TV includes: *Eastenders, Casualty, Stan, True Stories – Elizabeth Fry* (all BBC). Film includes *Where I Belong, Bloody Mary, All Friends Here* and *The Rat Trap*. Rebecca is a member of Teatro Vivo and Actors for Human Rights. Her first play *Sometimes I Laugh Like My Sister* has toured nationally, internationally and enjoyed a sell-out run at the Finborough. The show will tour South Africa in January-February 2013 and is published by Oberon Books.

Danny Scheinmann- Investigating Officer
Theatre includes: *Adelaide Road* (RSC), *Slave* (The Lowry), *The Play Of The Weather* (Hampton Court), *The Jollies* (Stephen Joseph Theatre), *Winter's Tale* (Bath Theatre Royal), *Ramayana* (National Theatre), *Quarantine* (Birmingham Rep), *Hansel Gretel Machine* (David Glass Ensemble, World Tour), *A Midsummer's Night Dream* (English Shakespeare Co), *Tempest, Measure for Measure, Taming of The Shrew, Much Ado* (all for A and BC). Film includes: *Monty Python Almost the Truth, Endgame, The Man Who Cried, Judas, The West Wittering Affair, Leon the Pig Farmer*. TV includes: *World Without End, Rosemary Thyme (ITV), Mile High (Sky), 99-1 (ITV), Sam Saturday (BBC)*. Danny is also a best selling novelist, his book "Random Acts of Heroic Love" was shortlisted for the Galaxy British Book Awards and has been translated in to 21 languages.

CREATIVE

Margarita Osepyan- Co-producer
Margarita has been working in the cultural sector since 1998 in the capacity of production coordinator, performer and then later producer for a number of international theatre and film festivals and companies in Russia and the UK. Credits include Russian Film Festival (2008), Behind the Wall season, Barbican (2009), Digital Stages Festival (2011). In 2009, she co-founded the independent events and production company GLAZ that initiates, curates and produces multidisciplinary cultural projects in London. Margarita has joined Sputnik Theatre Company in 2009 for the first Russian Theatre Festival in London (Soho Theatre, 2010).

takis- Set Designer
From 2007-2011 as Designer in residence for HighTide, takis built the visual identity of the company, designing diverse productions to great acclaim including the very successful STOVEPIPE in collaboration with the National Theatre (Off West End Design nomination), and DITCH with Old Vic. Theatre includes: *Fear* (Bush Theatre), *Bacchae* (Royal & Derngate), *Napoli* (West Yorkshire Playhouse & tour), *Clytemnestra & Measure for Measure* (Sherman Theatre), *Twelfth Night, As You Like It & Much Ado About Nothing* (Chester Open Air Theatre), *The Early Bird* (Finborough Theatre/ Project Art Centre-Dublin), *Signs of a Star Shaped Diva* (Theatre Royal Stratford East & tour), *Invasion* (Soho Theatre).

Ben Chessell- Video Designer
Ben studied Ecology and Medieval History at Melbourne University and graduated from Victorian College of the Arts in 2001. He works as a director and writer. Film

includes: *The Only Person In The World* (finalist at the 2002 Dendy Awards, nominated for an AFI award, won Best Short Film at the Australian Circle of Film Critics, *Heartworm, A Familiar Lullaby This Time In German, The Heartbreak Tour (SBSi)*. *The Heartbreak Tour, Little Deaths* project (Melbourne International Film Festival 2008). Television includes: *Dance Academy* (ABC TV Australia/ZDF Germany), *RUSH* and *Offspring* (Southern Star, Channel 10, Australia).

Charlie Lucas- Lighting Designer
Lighting designs include: *The Slow Sword* (Sputnik), *The Match Box* (Liverpool Playhouse), *The Magic Flute* (Garsington Opera at West Green House), *Mummyji Presents* (Watford Palace), *Walking the Tightrope* (Arcola), *Cautionary Tales* (Opera North), *Jealousy* (The Print Room), Red Riding Hood (Theatre Royal Stratford East), *Von Ribbentrop's Watch* (Oxford Playhouse and tour), *Red* (Robin Howard Dance Theatre, The Place), *Snakes and Ladders* (Brighton Pavilion Theatre), *1888* (Union Theatre), *I am a Camera* (Rosemary Branch Theatre), *Nina & Shaz* (Rich Mix and tour), *sohostreets* (Soho Theatre), *In Blood: The Bacchae* (Arcola). Charlie trained at RADA on the specialist stage electrics and lighting design course.

Ed Clarke- Sound Designer
Ed was nominated for an Olivier Award for his sound design for Danny Boyle's *Frankenstein* (National Theatre). Other sound designs include *Backbeat* (Duke of York's Theatre), *The Mysteries* and *The Good Hope* (National Theatre), *The Railway Children* (Waterloo International Station and Roundhouse Theatre Toronto), *FEAR* (Bush Theatre), *His Teeth* (Only Connect Theatre), *Happy Now?* (Hull Truck Theatre), *Sandi Toskvig's Christmas Cracker*

(Royal Festival Hall). As Associate Sound Designer: Matthew Bourne's *Early Adventures* (UK Tour), *Mary Poppins* (UK tour, Circustheatre Scheveningen and current US tour), *The Witches* (UK tour).

Bret Yount- Fight Director

Trained as an actor at the University of Arkansas and the Guildford School of Acting, Bret is currently a member of Equity's Fight Directors Register, a CT with the Society of American Fight Directors (SAFD) and a Master Teacher with the British Academy of Stage and Screen Combat (BASSC). Bret's fight direction work has been seen at: Playhouse Theatre, National Theatre, Royal Court Theatre, Royal Shakespeare Company, Hampstead Theatre, Liverpool Playhouse and Everyman, Haymarket Theatre-Basingstoke, Theatre-by-the-Lake, Keswick, Theatre Royal - York, Mercury Theatre- Colchester, Hull Truck Theatre, UCC - Singapore and the Palais des Festival, Cannes.

Lizzie Moore- Assistant Director

Lizzie is an Undergraduate at Oxford University, studying Russian and French. Theatre includes: *Julius Caesar* (RSC, ASM Work Placement and ASM- Newcastle Theatre Royal), *Peep* (Natural Shocks Theatre Company, Stage Manager). Lizzie also worked as ASM and Production Assistant on *I, Cinna* (Written and Directed by Tim Crouch)- an educational off-shoot to Greg Doran's *Julius Caesar*, which was filmed for a simultaneous broadcast in schools across the country.

PRODUCTION

Tim Highman on behalf of the Scenery Shop LLP- Production Manager
Tim is an extremely experienced Production Manager with twenty plus years in the entertainment industry gained at various levels. He has worked with numerous Theatre, Dance and Music companies throughout Europe and, most recently, for London 2012. Tim is also a founding partner of The Scenery Shop LLP; a London based specialist scenery construction / associated services business founded in 2010. The company has a wide range of clients includes Theatre, Dance and Opera Companies, Local Authorities, Event Companies, Private Clients and the Corporate Sector.

Nina Scholar- Stage Manager/DSM
Nina graduated from Queen Margaret College, Edinburgh in 1998 and has worked throughout the UK. Her previous work has been for companies including: The Royal Shakespeare Company; Birmingham Repertory Theatre; West Yorkshire Playhouse; Soho Theatre; New Wolsey Theatre; Hampstead Theatre; Bath Theatre Royal; Out of Joint; Liverpool Playhouse; Talawa; Setegaya Theatre, Tokyo; Theatre Royal Stratford East, The Players Theatre; The Tricycle; Hackney Empire.

Clare Amos- Wardrobe Supervisor
Recent work includes:
As Costume Designer: *Celebrity Night at Cafe Red* (Trafalgar Studios), *The Taming of the Shrew* (Aquila Theatre, US Tour), *The Day Shall Declare it*, *Wilderness for The Bush Bazaar* (Bush Theatre), *The Hit* (Hotel Indigo) (set and costume); *Translunar Paradise, The Big Smoke, Odyssey* (Theatre Ad Infinitum for Edinburgh Festival), and

international tours: *The Emperor Self* (En'kephale for Arcola Theatre), *Women of Manhattan* (The Old Red lion Theatre)
As Costume Supervisor: Grosvenor Park Open Air Theatre seasons with Chester Performs, 2010-2012; Hightide Festivals and transfers 2010-2011; *A Christmas Carol* (The Kings Head Theatre)

Claire Charlesworth- Technical ASM
Having graduated from Liverpool Institute for Performing Arts, Claire has worked with a wide range of companies both as a technician, stage manager and props team member. These companies include: Theatre Colwyn, ACC Liverpool, Chester Benson Productions, English National Opera, Men in Space, King's Head Theatre, Charles Court Opera. Claire also worked at the Olympic and Paralympic Ceremonies.

The production is produced by Sputnik Theatre Company
www.sputniktheatre.co.uk
Supported using public funding by Arts Council England, by
Garrick Charitable Trust and TNK-BP

Special thanks to New Diorama Theatre, David Byrne and
the team

and to
Tatiana Baskakova
Chris Eincomb
Natalia Magnitskaya
Ice&Fire Theatre Company
Amnesty International
Toynbee Studios
Pushkin House
Glas Publishing
Howard Gooding
Christine Bacon
GLAZ
Professor Bill Bowring
Valeriya Vygodnaya
Natalia Vartapetova
Olga Shirokostup
Society for Co-operation in Russian and Soviet Studies

One Hour Eighteen Minutes is a landmark in contemporary Russian playwriting. It is the first political play since 1991 which does not use changed identities or allegory – the playwright has decided to 'name names' of real life criminals. The play explores the largest known case of government corruption in modern Russian history – the theft of 230 million dollars orchestrated by two officials in the Interior Ministry, who were subsequently promoted. The story of how these same officers hid their crime is even more horrifying, and what makes this a truly disturbing and gripping play... *One Hour Eighteen* Minutes is inspired by a range of materials including first hand interviews with whistleblowers conducted by the playwright. Interestingly, some of these interviews were not included in the first version of the play which was produced in Russia in 2010. But a number of people who knew key characters in the play – happened to hear about it and watch it as audience members, and then approached the playwright, volunteering to provide additional testimony. These new interviews were included in an updated version of the play which is being produced simultaneously in Russia and in the UK, in November 2012.

Noah Birksted-Breen

Elena Gremina wishes to thank:
For gathering of documentary materials: Ekaterina Bondarenko, Nastya Patlay, Zosya Rodkevich
The materials also used in the play:
-diary and letters of Segrei Magnitsky
-materials from Natalya Magnitskaya and Tatiana Rudenko

- Report of the Public Observation Committee for Monitoring Compliance with Human Rights in places of forced detention (Head of Committee - Valery Borschev)
- Materials from Dmitry Myratov (Novaja Gazeta), Valery Borschev, Olga Romanova, Evgenija Albatz (Novoe Vremya) and Zoya Svetova

Gratitude for help to Marina Tokareva, Andrey Molchanov, Sergei Kalinin, Anna Karetnikova, Sergei Sokolov, Nikolai Gorokhov and, of course, to Natalia Nikolaevna Magnitskaya.

CHARACTERS

Vladimir- *Lawyer, colleague of Sergei Magnitsky*

Natasha Magnitskaya- *Magnitsky's Wife*

Natalia Nikolaevna Magnistkaya- *Magnitsky's Mother*

Lawyer- *At the same firm as Sergei*

Police Officer

Sergei's colleague

Elena Stashina- *Judge of the Tverskoi Court in Moscow*

Actor- *Questioning Judge Stashina*

Oleg Silchenko- *Investigating Officer, 32 years old in 2009*

Alexandra Gauss- *Military doctor in Sailors' Silence Prison*

Actor 1- *Based on an interview with Dr. Molchanov*

Actor 2

Lilia- *Lawyer, colleague of Sergei Magnitsky*

Sergei's Voice- *Voice of the late Sergei Magnitsky*

Prosecutor

Young Woman in The Ambulance

Sasha (m)- *A medical assistant in Prison*

The Guard

Actor with Kettle

Man- *Lowly prison official at the reception desk*

Irina Dudkina- *Interior Ministry Spokesperson*

Journalist

Home Office Official

This play is based on a true story. All characters in this play are based on real people. Many words in the play are a direct transcription of documentary sources – interviews, press conferences and court hearings. Where direct sources are not available, scenes have been dramatized, reconstructed or imagined, based on secondary sources.

Enter Vladimir.

VLADIMIR. Sergei was the most brutal type of lawyer I have ever known. Everything which wasn't written into the law didn't exist for Sergei. Some people say he wasn't a real lawyer because he didn't have a legal diploma, but forget all that, he was a most brilliant lawyer. He could charm everyone – though I've also heard that he sometimes shouted at subordinates if they couldn't understand something which he thought was simple.

Enter Natasha.

NATASHA. Sergei and I were in the same class when we were 15 years old. He was always at the top of his class. He was very popular – a leader, but not the kind who pushes others down. He always let his schoolmates copy his homework. Perhaps that will sound wrong to people in

1

England? Everyone does that in Russia – if you get good marks, you share your essays with your friends – I did it too. After school, he moved to Moscow and we split up. He went to the Plekhanov Institute and got honours with a silver medal. He would have got gold but... he was distracted by the girls in Moscow. Five years later, he came back to our home town, Nalchik, in the south of Russia, and he asked to see me. He came to my house and asked if I'd like to go for a walk. He'd had his fill of Moscow girls. He asked me straight away to come and live with him. I came to stay with him for a week – then a month after that I moved to Moscow for good. It didn't matter that we'd both made mistakes when we were young. For the next thirteen years – every day was like a honey moon.

VLADIMIR. He worked a lot so he didn't have much time for his family during the week. When everyone left the office, around 10pm, he'd start doing the really important work which needed his full concentration...

NATASHA. He loved making model planes and tanks with his older son. And he doted on his younger son – to the point where he was completely irrational. Nikita would be making some baby noises – and Sergei would say – 'Did you hear that? He just said *fish*'! I'd say – 'there's no way he said fish'– and he'd say - 'He definitely said fish'! And he wrote down every word which our son learnt to say in a little notebook.

Exit Vladimir and Natasha. Enter Natalia.

SERGEI'S MOTHER. When I pulled back the sheet, in the morgue, I saw that all the bones in my son's hands were broken. I don't know if post-mortem protocol means they're meant to look at that and record it. But I'd like an explanation for that – was Sergei knocking on his cell door for help or was he struggling to get away from somebody? I don't know if the state autopsy is meant to record that. They wouldn't let us organise an independent autopsy.

Exit Natalia.

An office. Knocking at the door. A lawyer goes to open up.

She sees a large group of plain clothes police outside the door.

LAWYER. What's going on? Who are you?

POLICE OFFICER. Get them out of their offices.

LAWYER. You can't do that. I'm calling the police

POLICE OFFICER. We have a warrant to search the premises.

She *looks at the warrant and the police ID*

LAWYER. Look, we haven't been notified about a search –

POLICE OFFICER. We'll start with Sergei Magnitsky's office.

LAWYER. He's not in yet.

POLICE OFFICER. Okay, we'll start with your office. (*The police officer grabs his arm*)

VLADIMIR. Both my parents were lawyers, I heard them talking about clients' issues at home from the age of 4, so that's where I learnt the law much more than at university. I was a researcher in politics and history when the financial crash happened in the mid-90s, and it was impossible to earn enough to feed my family, so I moved into law. It turned out I was a strange creature – first, I'd been an expert in law among political scholars, now I was an expert in politics among lawyers. Sergei also learned the law at home.

In another time and place, we hear Vladimir's doorbell ringing.

The policeman has a file in his hands.

POLICE OFFICER. Tell me about this one.

LAWYER. I refuse to talk to you until my lawyer arrives.

POLICE OFFICER. *(Hesitates, to another officer by phone)* She says she won't talk without a lawyer present - do I wait? I don't know. *(To Lawyer)* How long will it take?

LAWYER. I don't know.

POLICE OFFICER. She doesn't know.

POLICE OFFICER. (*Waving the file*) Your client hasn't paid their full taxes – you need to give me any –

LAWYER. Are you serious? Do you know what this is? A piece of paper from the Federal Ministry of Finance explicitly stating that the right amount of tax has been paid by my client!

POLICE OFFICER. Yeah? Well, I'm taking this with me. (*Takes it*).

LAWYER. My client even declared their off-shore tax.

POLICE OFFICER. Why would anyone do that?

LAWYER. Not everyone's corrupt.

POLICE OFFICER. I need all your files relating to any company you represent which has paid a large amount of tax in the last year.

LAWYER. Your warrant only names one company.

POLICE OFFICER. Give me those fucking files.

The police officer picks the lawyer up by the throat and lowers him down onto the floor, then beats him brutally. Another lawyer runs in and he has a camera or phone to record the beating.

LAWYER 2. Hey!

POLICE OFFICER. (*To the lawyer who has run in*) She pulled a gun on me. Do you know how many years she'd get for that? So you'd better keep your mouth shut...

Exeunt.

It's midnight. Sergei's colleague has finally managed to wake up Vladimir, through his persistent door bell ringing efforts. Vladimir lets Sergei's colleague into his hallway.

SERGEI'S COLLEAGUE. I hope I didn't wake up your wife?

VLADIMIR. Our favourite saying in this household is - if you can afford to switch your phone off at night, then you're not a real lawyer. How can I help?

SERGEI'S COLLEAGUE. Look, I'll keep it brief. It's much more serious this time –

VLADIMIR. You know I'm not trained in criminal law.

SERGEI'S COLLEAGUE. We have 14 of the best criminal barristers from the West – but this is Russia. Look you won't be officially named on the case. Did you ever meet Sergei? He'll do all the field work... you'll be the scorpion behind the scenes...

VLADIMIR. What's the situation right now?

SERGEI'S COLLEAGUE. Well, basically, we've got nothing. We know the name of the police who raided the office –

VLADIMIR. What did they take?

SERGEI'S COLLEAGUE. 20 to 30 boxes of files –

VLADIMIR. Your official documents and company seals?

SERGEI'S COLLEAGUE. Yes.

VLADIMIR. Has anyone tried to use the seals?

SERGEI'S COLLEAGUE. They've asked us to meet them for an 'informal discussion' to discuss mutually agreeable 'terms' for getting our files back, obviously we said no... so it's stalemate.

VLADIMIR. Call me if there are any new developments.

SERGEI'S COLLEAGUE. Do you know how many cases we lost before you started advising us.

VLADIMIR. 35.

SERGEI'S COLLEAGUE. I'll keep asking if I have to – tomorrow – next week – the week after...

VLADIMIR. I don't switch my phone off – but I do know how to block numbers...

Exeunt.

ITEM ONE – THE JUDGE

Enter Judge Elena Stashina, who extended Sergei's pre-trial detention and refused him medical care, four days before he died.

ACTOR. (*Reads out loud*). Questions for Judge Elena Stashina. In his diary, Magnitsky wrote: "I sent a complaint that I hadn't been given access to a kettle even though they know that the water in prison isn't clean enough to drink without boiling it first. I was without drinkable water or warm food, for 38 hours. Judge Elena Stashina said that handing out cups of boiling water was not her responsibility." Do you deny this accusation?

STASHINA. It isn't my responsibility. My responsibility is to judge. I'm a good judge.

ACTOR. A good judge?

STASHINA. Yes - one million prisoners. Because we work hard.

ACTOR. Have you ever been late for a court proceeding?

STASHINA. No, I always arrive on time.

ACTOR. How do you cope with draughts in your court room? Do you have some favourite woollen leggings? Or perhaps a warm shawl?

STASHINA. The proceedings take place behind closed doors. There aren't any draughts.

ACTOR. Has anyone in your family fought in a war? What did they tell you about war?

STASHINA. Someone in my family fought in a war. Yes, they told me about it.

ACTOR. Which war song do you like the most? Can you sing it?

STASHINA. (*Singing*) Our huge country is rising, Is rising for deathly battle.

ACTOR. Do you cook soft-boiled or hard-boiled eggs in the morning?

STASHINA. I use "boil in the bag" eggs.

ACTOR. Did you collect sweet wrappers as a child? Did you prefer the brightly-coloured wrappers or the shiny foil ones?

STASHINA. I preferred the foil ones.

ACTOR. Were you taken to the seaside as a child? Did you prefer pebbles or sand?

STASHINA. Pebbles.

ACTOR. Did you go to nursery?

STASHINA. Yes

ACTOR. Did the boys there pull your hair?

STASHINA. Yes

ACTOR. What was the nickname of your childhood friend?

STASHINA. Vika

STASHINA. Did your Mother plait your hair in the mornings?

ACTOR. No, my Grandmother did

ACTOR. Can you finish the nursery rhyme "How now, greedy cow..."?

ACTOR. Did you have a favourite toy?
STASHINA. Yes...

Long pause. Looks into the auditorium.

STASHINA. If you want to understand whether I'm a flesh-and-blood human being why didn't you just ask me directly?

No. I'm not a person. Judges are not "people" in the legal process. We reflect the will of the government.

I've had cases where there was not enough evidence against the accused– but I managed to get a guilty verdict in the end. That's my job. If you're in court and the Judge says black is white and white is black, then that's how it has to be.

Exeunt.

Vladimir is on the phone.

VLADIMIR. Okay, okay, listen... listen... Sergei? Listen to me now! You're listening to me? Calm down. Okay. Are you calm? I understand what you're saying – but we can't talk about whether it's likely, or good, or credible, or probable, from now on we need to start asking – 'is it possible'. Look, I'm willing to share your optimism in the law – that's why I took this case on, I love stupid cases, the more stupid the better, - it's the stupid cases I can't resist – but I'm missing information. We need to meet in person or I can't move this forward...

Exit Vladimir.

ITEM TWO – THE INVESTIGATING OFFICER

Oleg Silchenko, investigating officer. Responsible for interrogating Sergei Magnisky

INVESTIGATING OFFICER. It's easy to make beautiful speeches and feel a righteous anger. But I investigate – I wasn't responsible for the conditions of his detention.

Magnitsky was a lawyer for the thieves. It's spelt "businessman" – it's pronounced "thief". Have you seen the endless zeros in their off-shore accounts? Because I have.

What does that mean - "a hired lawyer"? I'm also "hired". So what have I done wrong? Anyway, I get it. It's because Magnitsky's now become a Nelson Mandela, a poster boy for capitalism and basically a ray of light in medieval Russia. Don't make me laugh. Companies like the one Magnitsky worked for have carried anything worth anything out of my fucking country into your fucking country.

Yes, he did say he was in pain. That's why he should have co-operated with the investigation. But not him. 230

15

million dollars has gone missing from the state budget – a fraudulent tax rebate by the company he represents - but he won't talk about that.

And then there's the petitions he loved to write: (*He leafs through some papers.*) "Men who've been recently arrested are not given cells immediately." I didn't know you were coming here for a holiday. "They didn't give me access to boiling water, 14th September. They didn't give me access to boiling water, 13th September." It's a strange sequence, 14th then 13th. As if it's all, I don't know, made up...?

"They keep moving me from cell to cell. This cell has no glass in the windows; up to 70 people are living together in one small space, of 20 square metres. Many detainees smoke. It's extremely difficult to breathe. There are toilets in some cells but they aren't separated from the main part of the cell. In another cell, the toilet was just a hole in the floor." So?

"Rats are running around through the sewerage system. Some of my cell mates and I stuffed a plastic bottle in the toilet, but a rat gnawed through it and came up into our

16

cell anyway." Go out into Moscow – to any market place or building site... there's rats running right under your feet. Are you gonna write petitions about that?

"On the same day that I filed a new petition, they moved me to a cell where the conditions of detainment were far worse even than they'd been up to that point. The floor was flooded with sewerage, it was impossible to move around the cell, except by jumping from bed to bed."

"Last night, they put a mentally disturbed man in our cell." This is science fiction.
"During my stay in the Butyrky prison, I was brought to pre-trial hearings four times, and each time, I was subjected to rough treatment, bordering on torture." (*Laughs*.) So, do you see what I mean? 450 petitions in eleven months. Well, it's pretty obvious he was preparing it for Strasbourg.

But I responded appropriately to his bullshit! (*Reads out his reply*.) "I am writing to inform you that your petition of the 19th of August 2009, in defense of the interests of the accused, S. Magnitsky, in which you ask the investigator to address the Head of the Moscow Directorate of the Federal Penal Service, Detention Centre-77, block 2, Moscow, Russia, about the need to provide ultrasound examination of the abdominal cavity of the accused, S. Magnitsky, held in detention, has been considered, and on the 31st of August 2009, a decree has been issued with a complete rejection of that request. Current legislation does not lay responsibility on the investigating officer to oversee health conditions of the accused, held in detention."

But now, people are popping up, saying - "I killed him". I made it clear to him all along, he needed to retract his false statements and start naming names.

Exit Investigating Officer. Enter Vladimir.

VLADIMIR. The authorities got worried when Sergei decided to speak to the press, in November 2008 – and Business Week published an article suggesting credible links between the police, the stolen company and a fraudulent tax claim for 230 million dollars. They started to come after all the lawyers involved in one by one. My flat was surrounded by police. Not too pleasant. We lived on the 1st floor. So, you know, you have agents listening in with antennae in front of your windows 24/7, you look out of the window, so they move 5 metres to the side, and then wait a bit till they can move back... They did an imitation robbery in my apartment, they turned everything upside down, and they also searched my office when I wasn't there. But I'm not the kind of guy who leaves confidential papers lying around, so all they found was one big file with my name and address in it.

In my family, it was my son Misha who was fighting to leave Russia. I said to him 'shut up, I'm the one who decides in this family, your job is to get ready for your last year at school'. At breakfast one morning, he said, 'Dad, forget about yourself for a minute. If a client comes to you and tells you the whole story of what's happening to you, what would your advice to him be?' I said 'My professional intuition is – he should leave Russia immediately'. Then my son said – 'so behave professionally'. I thought I was different because I was an adviser to the head of the Constitutional Court, and an adviser to the Mayor of Moscow, I was counting on being different from others. I spoke to people in the Duma, the Parliament, but nobody could help. I couldn't get used to the idea that nobody could do anything for me.

The police called me in for questioning at 8pm on a Saturday. I said to my colleague 'What's that all about?' He said 'You won't be able to file a complaint over the weekend, so they can do what they want with you, at least until Monday morning.'

Exit Vladimir.

ITEM THREE – THE DOCTOR

Alexandra Gauss. The last doctor to examine Sergei before he died.

GAUSS. Magnitsky was complaining about acute stomach pains. It could have been true, but it might not have been. They always lie... they raise their temperature. They pretend to faint. One guy put lead from an indelible pencil in his eyes to give himself burns. Another bashed his head against the wall. The main thing is not to show fear, then they stop trying to pressure you psychologically.

We've all got flak because of him – but it's just because Magnitsky is now this famous guy and everyone talks about this one case.

He had a fit... out of the blue. He shouted, as if he was in pain. He got hysterical. I called the emergency team, I told them to give him a small injection and I went back upstairs to my office. Then they phoned me and said: "The patient is lying on the floor, his physical condition is uncertain." I didn't hear from them for another hour and eighteen minutes.

You have to think about this rationally. It's dangerous for us to be here. Just look at this. The walls in all the cells are dirty. You can't clean them if you try. (*Tests it with a finger.*) What's this? Huh? You think this is dust? Tuberculosis. You think it's dirt? Hepatitis. If a prisoner bites you, you get AIDS. That's happened. Did you know prison doctors are paid three times less than normal doctors?

The so-called investigators lock people up here to persuade them to give the right testimony instead of investigating properly - and we're meant to be responsible for their health. Suddenly we're "guilty" when someone dies. I can account for every single minute of my time. I was following orders.

Look, the duty of a qualified doctor in prison is to expose fakers. How come he was fine before? He came here and suddenly he started getting stomach pains?

He did request an examination but look – what I'm saying is - why? It clearly states in the records that he'd already had treatment the month before. So, I explained it to him very clearly: "When you get out of here, you'll get all the treatment you need. You're in prison. Nobody has to provide for you. You think we're going to treat you every month!"

Exit Gauss. Vladimir is on the phone.

VLADIMIR. Julia where are you? Is Misha with you? Look, you need to go home immediately. Leave the beetroot. Go home, pack a bag and meet me at Sheremetievo. Get there by 9pm. And don't switch the light on in the flat. It's ok, I left the visas open.
He hangs up. He makes another call.

Two actors enter to prepare for the reconstruction of Item Five.

Exit Vladimir.

ITEM FOUR - RECONSTRUCTION

Actor 1's body is used as a forensic model for the Actor 2's medical explanations.

ACTOR 1. The acute pancreatitis spreads quickly. The pancreas is dying so there's a discharge of enzymes. This leads to poisoning and there are very sharp bouts of pain. It's not possible to compare it with anything else. You try to relieve your body as much as you can, you lie on your right hand side so as not to pressure the pancreas.

The afflicted person can't even straighten their legs because their abdominal wall is pulled tight. They'll lie in this position, with bent legs, - in the foetal position.

The muscles here (*under the solar plexus*) contract, trying to protect the gland.

The doctor tries to touch the patient but the patient tries to move away from any physical contact, because it's so painful - his stomach is like a pumped-up tyre. I mean, this whole muscular top part is trying to shut the whole thing down. If you don't have an operation within 5-6 hours, you die.

You're trying not to move at all, you just sort of inch yourself around. If you were having a heart attack, you worry that you were going to die and start panicking, but with pancreatitis, you lie down and it's (*In a rasping voice*) "nobody fucking touch me".

They leave. Enter Vladimir. As he talks, banging at a door escalates in volume.

VLADIMIR. When I got out, they turned their attention to another lawyer in the investigation, Eduard. Eduard is a tough nut. He just disappeared like James Bond. Nobody had any idea where he was – he escaped to Siberia and became an illegal. A month later, he turned up in South Korea – asking for us to wire him money.

(*The banging is now loud.*) Lilia, another lawyer, was woken up by police at 8am.

LILIA. (*Looks through the peephole of her door, then picks up her mobile and walks into the bathroom*) Mum – how are the cats? (*She starts putting on her make-up*). It's um... don't panic when I say this - but I'm about to be arrested...Mum? No – I haven't done anything – it's to do with work... (*The banging has stopped*). I'll call you when I know where they're taking me... I'm going to hang up now okay, I've got to go. I love you. Ok, ok bye mum. (*She opens her door and walks out*).

VLADIMIR. Lilia wasn't a woman to meet twenty men without make up but she took so long putting it on they assumed she wasn't home. When she realised the coast was clear, she ran for it – and hopped on a train to the Ukraine. Everyone else ran away but Sergei played by the rules. That was his problem. He even continued the investigation and discovered that this wasn't the first time they police had organized a fraudulent tax claim. And they followed him step by step.

Enter Natasha. Vladimir leaves.

NATASHA. I had just taken our youngest son to the doctor, early. I arrived back home to find they were searching the flat. Sergei was still at there. He often worked late but he loved to sleep in in the morning. He was like anyone else in that way. I could see the search was making him nervous but he kept saying 'nothing to worry about – it's just a search'. And actually it wasn't like they were tipping things over. In Russian, for a search like this there has to be two independent witnesses. And yes there were these two girls sitting on our bed the whole time but the weird thing was they were chatting and laughing with the police officers. We were told to feed our children but we weren't allowed to do anything else. They were there until two in the morning. When I realised that they were taking Sergei with them, he said 'Don't worry, I'll be home tomorrow'. And that was...

Exit Natasha. Inside a court hearing. We hear Sergei's voice – and we see the Judge, Prosecutor and Investigating Officer. The Prosecutor is reading a newspaper throughout the proceeding.

JUDGE. Magnitsky, please.

SERGEI. Part 1 of Article 19, Part 3 of Article 123 of the Constitution of the Russian Federation, Part 4 of Article

15 of the Criminal Code require the provision of equality between Parties, coming before the court, yet unlike the prosecution, I must be present in court in a cage similar to cages in which wild animals are kept....

Time Passes.

SERGEI. The permitted limitation of rights and freedom in my case is not in accordance with Part 3 of Article 55 of the Constitution of the Russian Federation and there is no basis for it in Federal Law, and for that reason I respectfully ask the court...

Time Passes.

SERGEI. In accordance with Subclause B Point 3 Article 6 of the convention of the rights of the individual, I should be permitted sufficient time and opportunity to read new materials in my case. I was told about these 300 pages of accusations at 5 am this morning...

JUDGE. Prosecutor?

PROSECUTOR. Your Honour, Magnisky is being detained in accordance with the decision of the district court. I leave it to your discretion.

JUDGE. Investigating officer?

INVESTIGATING OFFICER. Your Honour, I object because I consider this to be a tactical and unnecessary delay of the judicial process.

JUDGE. The court has conferred onsite and rejects Magnisky's petition.

Exeunt. Enter Vladimir, Natasha and Natalia.

VLADIMIR. When Sergei was first in prison, it sounded romantic like when Lenin was in jail and he wrote his book... They hadn't make a decision to destroy him right away so for the first few weeks, conditions were more or less appropriate.. Sergei wrote complaints for all other prisoners, whether they were innocent shopkeepers or street gangsters. We all thought – he's fine, he's still cracking jokes. He was strong. When he became ill, he kept it to himself. That made it a lot worse for him.

SERGEI'S MOTHER. Whenever Sergei complained about something in prison, they
told him 'File a petition'. So he did, but when he filed the petitions, they ignored them. Sergei kept asking them for the most basic things. Was it really so hard to bring him some warm clothes and blankets so he wouldn't get worse?

NATASHA. Before he was in prison, he hadn't been to see a doctor in years – the worst he ever had was a headache. In prison, he kept getting colds, bronchitis –

SERGEI'S MOTHER. And then the stomach pains started...

VLADIMIR. The very fact that Sergei kept a diary in prison and wrote all those petitions - that's a heroic action. When you come to prison, you need to think of the worst thing that could happen and say to yourself 'it's already happened'. You need to forget about your previous life.

Though of course that's impossible — especially for an intelligent man - you think about why it happened.

SERGEI'S MOTHER. The wife of a former prisoner spoke to us. Her husband knew Sergei in prison. She said that sometimes when it all got too much, Sergei would turn to face the wall, and lean his forehead against it for a while, like he was concentrating, or just trying to shut everything else out.

NATASHA. We asked to visit him in prison but they always refused.

SERGEI'S MOTHER. We only ever saw him at the court hearings.

NATASHA. We couldn't speak to him. If we went over to him, the guard said — 'get back'. We could see him at a distance. So we could wave and smile.

SERGEI'S MOTHER. Once, they told us — lots of the prison staff are on holiday at the moment so there's no way we can pass on your letters. We had to pass messages through his lawyer. We told him 'we're waiting for you, we love you, the children are fine, how are you, are they feeding you properly'...

NATASHA. Sergei asked to use the phone to speak to his children. They told him – we'd be happy to give you permission but the prison isn't technically equipped for that.

SERGEI'S MOTHER. I wrote him a letter asking him: Sergei how do you feel? Please tell me what symptoms you have, so I can ask my doctor friend to give us advice. I didn't think he'd reply to that, but when I got his letter with a very detailed description of his stomach pains, I understood this is serious, and that's when I got really worried.

NATASHA. Every day we hoped he'd be allowed out of prison. Hope left us bit by bit, but what can you do? People always hope for a miracle...

SERGEI'S MOTHER. They never charged my son with any crime. They just tried to break him down over time.

VLADIMIR. Sergei never gave in. He's not that kind of person. Even in the last few days, he wrote several petitions...

Exeunt.

ITEM FIVE – GIRL ON THE FRONT SEAT OF THE AMBULANCE

The young woman is on the front seat of a civilian ambulance.

YOUNG WOMAN. What's it got to do with me?

I don't even know why I was summoned.

I didn't look round.

The radio was on. That's why I didn't hear anything. Look, if there's one person who's got nothing to do with this, you're looking at her.

I don't know.

I can't remember.

Okay. The prisoner sat with guards on the back seat.

Prison and me - we're from two totally different worlds.

They call us over sometimes because we have a small depot

for the ambulances not far from the prison. I've always managed to avoid those sorts of places.

I don't know why he died. It wasn't on my watch.

Look, I mean, do you ever drive past either of those prisons? Well you don't know anything about them, right? And it's exactly the same for me. I have the right to know nothing.

Everyone knows he died from acute pancreatitis... What are you suggesting?

Who told you that I turned the radio up?

Sergei's mother enters. Vladimir enters.

NATALIA. 13 October 2009. I took out Shakespeare from the prison library: Hamlet, Macbeth, Othello, King Lear. Only Othello and Desdemona's death touched me, all the other heroes die because of money. Or they die quietly, like Ophelia. Or by being tricked, like Hamlet. By the way, some pages had been torn out of *Hamlet*, including the pages with the famous "To be or not to be" soliloquy. So I'll have to re-read the full text again when I'm home.

JOURNALIST. We'd been strongly advised by lawyers to redact certain elements of hte following scene.

VLADIMIR. This is Mr... He works for Russian ministry of...
According to some people, soon after the 6 billion went missing - and right around the time Sergei was put in prison - his lifestyle was becoming excessive.

He went to the poshest Moscow clubs, he traveled to.., and to... and he also made a two week trip to...

but that's all we're are allowed to say.

Exit Vladimir

NATALIA. "Today I was thinking of grandma. Her birthday must have been one of these days. Don't worry too much about me. Sometimes I surprise myself by how well I feel: everything seems perfectly easy, I just miss you all and I miss being at home."

Exeunt Vladimir.

ITEM SIX – THE MEDICAL ASSISTANT

Sasha pulls his phone out of his pocket and fidgets with it. He's outside the cell where Magnitsky died. There are dull thuds and screams coming from the inside.

SASHA. It was packed, even without me. The emergency team just calms them down with them down with a small injection, that's all.

Look, I don't know. Why you asking me anyway? I've already been questioned.

Who knows what was wrong with him. I think it was an inflammation of bullshit.

(*Looking back at his mobile.*) Seriously, though, is it normal that a mobile can't read the SIM card? Sometimes it can, sometimes it can't!

I bought a Siemens instead of a Nokia 'cos it's red. And *hello*! I read on a blog that they're out of date. It upsets me: nothing lasts forever. Not so long ago Siemens was cool and Nokia wasn't. And now? Basically, Siemens is shit. The vibration is weak, I don't feel it in my pocket when I'm walking. Or it suddenly freezes, is that normal?

On the other hand... 3G!!! (*Disappointed*) But Nokia has a better ringtone, it's louder anyways, 'cos the speaker's sick...

Look - you highlight what you need to delete, press the buttons and – easy as that. Me, I don't delete things, I make a new folder and stick everything in there, what if you suddenly need it later?

But hey - polyphonic ringtone! It's almost a smartphone. It can do anything. Beauty! (*Pressing the buttons.*) Oh yeah baby! I take it all back!

A normal doctor doesn't work in a prison. I'm a medical assistant and I don't plan on becoming a doctor, by the way. You think I'm gonna study six years to become a doctor? No way. Just getting out of military service is enough for me.

(*Presses buttons on his phone. Something annoys him.*) Come on! Don't freeze on me again -

Then one of the guards from the emergency group comes out.

SASHA. That was quick. What happened?

THE GUARD. He's dead.

SASHA. Ri-ght... Okay....

GUARD. Woah – that's a beauty! I love red phones...

SASHA. (*Trying to turn off the phone but it keeps ringing.*) Thanks, man. Oh no – I can't shut it up!... I shouldn't have bought the fucking Siemens.

ITEM SEVEN - THE JUDGE CONDEMNED

In real life, Judge Stashina is still alive. But in this play, we've just killed her off.

STASHINA. Please, a cup of boiling water, I need to something drink. I'm not asking for an end to all my suffering. I understand that this is just the beginning. Just one cup.

Listen. I'm so tired. I'm only asking for the most basic things.

Natasha walks up to a counter, a kind of tiny window at the perimeter of the prison.

NATASHA. Magnitsky, Sergei.

MAN. Wait there.

NATASHA. I've brought him some medicine.

39

MAN. He's been moved back to the Sailors' Silence prison. You need to go there and ask for him.

NATASHA. How come we were never informed - (*The man shuts the counter*).

STASHINA. Okay, fine – I'll pay for it, how much are you asking.

(*She digs in his pockets.*) There. Just give it to me quickly!

She waits.
Natasha walks up to a counter, a kind of tiny window at the perimeter of the prison.

NATASHA. Magnitsky, Sergei.

MAN. He's been moved to another cell – ask over there. (*He shuts the counter*).

Natasha walks up to a counter, a kind of tiny window at the perimeter of the prison.

NATASHA. Magnitsky, Sergei.

MAN. Hang on.

NATASHA. Look – I don't understand what's going on – I'm trying to find out about my husband –

MAN. Yes, I have some information about his location. He's dead. (*The man shuts the counter*).

NATASHA. What did you say?…

Actor brings in a kettle with boiling water.

STASHINA. What can I pour it into? Look, this isn't funny!

Do you have a cup? Or something plastic at least?

Natasha walks up to a counter, a kind of tiny window at the perimeter of the prison.

NATASHA. Magnitsky, Sergei. I'm trying to find out -

The man shuts the counter.

STASHINA. I'd give more if I had anything. They took my watch…

I've given everything I have…

Stashina puts her hands out towards the kettle, cupping her hands to try to catch some water.

Boiling water is poured over his hands.

She shouts from pain.

Natasha collects some flowers which she puts on Sergei's grave.

VLADIMIR. Sergei was two weeks away from the legal limit for detention without trial. Nobody was going to be able to stop him testifying in open court. We can't reconstruct exactly what happened at the end. But what we know for certain is that eight guards took him into a separate cell and beat him severely. Then they gave him a type of injection which hasn't been seen in Russia for a hundred years. The official line was that he died of complications from diabetes but they destroyed his blood samples which were taken as required by law. They tried to make Sergei's corpse suit their story. The staged post mortem recorded three lungs. But nobody talks about that. Sergei didn't have three lungs. I believe they replaced some of his organs to hide their crimes.

Exit Vladimir.

ITEM EIGHT THE PRESS ROOM

At the Press Room of the Russian Interior Ministry.

DUDKINA. Ladies and gentlemen of the press. I can now report a new development in the case of the missing 5 billion roubles, or 230 million dollars, of public money. We now have conclusive evidence that Sergei Magnitsky was responsible for the theft. We have sworn testimony from an individual which makes this incontrovertible. The missing link is Mr. Gasanov – who was instructed in everything he did by Sergei Magnitsky. We haven't been able to speak to Mr. Gasanov – but we know about this link as a matter of fact because someone working for Mr. Gasanov, called Mr. Markelov, has confirmed the whole story. Any questions?

JOURNALIST. Can you say what relationship Mr. Markelov had to Mr. Gasanov?

DUDKINA. Markelov was one of the criminal gang. He met Gasanov in December last year. Gasanov instructed Markelov in everything he did – he handed Markelov the company seals in person on the 15th of December. And Gasanov went with Markelov to the notary office to re-register the stolen company into Markelov's name on the 17th of December. Any questions?

Time passes.

Enter Vladimir. A phone call comes in on Vladimir's phone.

VLADIMIR. Hello. Hello.

He looks at it warily. He puts the phone on the table.

VLADIMIR. Leaving Russia was disastrous for me. I'm a specialist of Russian law which nobody needs here. Now that I'm London, it's like - everything I did in my life is nothing. I spent 30 years of my life for something that is bullshit. I need to choose another profession, medicine, or biology, but not the law because that doesn't work. I rely on somebody else's charity to get by.

Exit Vladimir, leaving his phone on the table. Back at the Press Room.

Someone is whispering in the Journalist's ear.

DUDKINA. (*Pointing to a journalist*) Yes.

JOURNALIST. We have found evidence that Gasanov died on 2nd of October last year which means that 15th of December, Markelov must have gone to Gasanov's grave to collect the seals – and Gasanov must have turned up as a ghost at the notary office on the 17th of December. Your comments?

Dudkina leafs manically through her papers.

Time passes.

A text message arrives on Vladimir's phone.
"If history teaches us one thing, it's that anybody can be killed. Michael Corleone"

Back at the Press Room.

DUDKINA. More proof has emerged which demonstrates that it was definitely Magnitsky to blame. A convicted thief Mr. Kurochkin – also one of the criminal gang - has given us his testimony – confirming the link between Gasanov and Magnitsky. Kurochkin was told in no uncertain terms by Gasanov that the mastermind of the whole affair was Magnitsky.

JOURNALIST. Will Kurochkin face an open court hearing?

DUDKINA. No, because shortly after we spoke to Mr Kurochkin, he travelled to Ukraine – and just outside the airport he got acute cirrhosis of the liver and died.

JOURNALIST. Died?

DUDKINA. Yes

JOURNALIST. Do you intend to discount his testimony since it can't be independently verified, now that he's dead?

DUDKINA. No – we just consider ourselves fortunate to have spoken to him before his sudden demise. Any other questions?

JOURNALIST. Is there any progress on recovering the stolen money?

Time passes.

A text message arrives on Vladimir's phone.
"There's a lawyer who died in prison, very interesting case.
No good will come of speaking out against it."

At the Press Room.

DUDKINA. I can now confirm that the stolen money was taken by a new suspect called Mr. Korobeinikov. He's a former underwear salesman turned banker - who became the owner of the Universal Savings Bank where all the money was deposited. And no – we can't speak to him – because he died falling off the 3rd floor balcony of a penthouse which he'd just bought.

JOURNALIST. So – that means you know where the money is – and it will be returned to the Russian public?

Time passes.

Vladimir at the Home Office in London.

HOME OFFICE OFFICIAL. (H*e looks at Vladimir's phone and hands it back to him*) Sorry to keep you waiting. I've looked into this and um – well, let me explain.

VLADIMIR. May I interrupt you there? I don't want to be here –

HOME OFFICE OFFICIAL. Yes, I'd rather be in Spain myself!

VLADIMIR. My former client insisted that I come. I'm a lawyer – so I understand that the Home Office can't do anything for me unless I'm actually murdered on the streets of London.

HOME OFFICE OFFICIAL. I'm afraid that's true.

VLADIMIR. And it's your protocol to advise me to be careful.

HOME OFFICE OFFICIAL. Yes, exactly. I'm glad we have such a good understanding.

VLADIMIR. Please consider your task complete.

HOME OFFICE OFFICIAL. At least for the time being, eh?! (*He realizes the joke is in poor taste*). Sorry. Here, let me give you one of our brochures about how to stay safe. It's full of really good tips.

Exeunt Vladimir and Home Office official. Dudkina looks manically through her papers, an advisers brings her a new piece of paper.

DUDKINA. Ladies and gentlemen of the press. I can now report a new development in the Magnitsky case and the missing 5 billion roubles. All of the bank records relating to this case were in a van which crashed and exploded in 2008.

JOURNALIST. That was two years ago

DUDKINA. Therefore the case has now been closed. I won't be taking questions.

Exit Dudkina.

HOME OFFICE OFFICIAL. And did you drive here today?

VLADIMIR. Yes

HOME OFFICE OFFICIAL. Well that's a good place to start. Every time you drive you need to check your car. Have a good look underneath. If you see anything hanging down...

VLADIMIR. Don't get in it?

HOME OFFICE OFFICIAL. Yes! Its lovely to deal with a bright chap.

Enter Vladimir.

VLADIMIR. If I travelled to Russia now, they wouldn't bother with an accusation or an arrest, they'd just kidnap me... We know our opponents by name. And they have hundreds of agents, we're fighting with one of the strongest intelligence agencies in the world. They know everything about us, where we live, what we're doing. It's exhausting because you think about this 24 hours a day. You can't imagine how much I want to think about something else.

Enter Sergei's mother.

SERGEI'S MOTHER. They have reopened the case against Sergei. They're doing it to show that anyone who stands up for him is defending a criminal. It turns out that everyone involved was promoted. They sent me a summons. "In case of a failure to appear in court, you will face a fine or forcible custody. They're saying, he's your son so you're answerable for his crimes.

NATASHA. A friend of mine is a photographer and made a huge photo of Sergei like this (*she indicates*) which we have on the wall. That's how we remember him. Of course, we remember him every minute of every day. Our oldest son was 8 when it all happened. He kept saying: if only I had a magic wand, I'd make this whole situation right. I'd tele-transport the people who are doing this to dad onto another planet.

Curtain